Mini MUSIC BOOK 1

Songs written by:

____

(YOUR NAME HERE!)

Created By: Zachary Seckman
Catalog: KDP-MMB1-PC
ZSMUSIC PUBLISHING
music made just for you

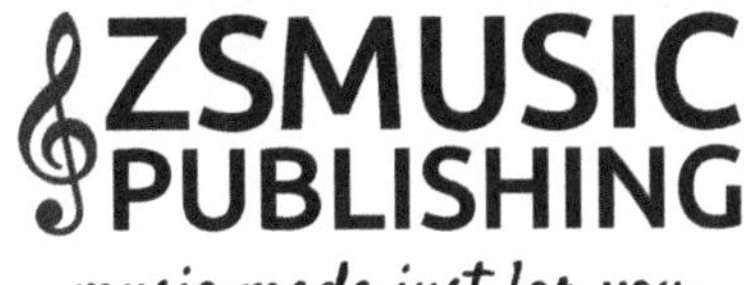

Through the MINI MUSIC books, students are introduced to various concepts through composition. In Book 1, students write 66 short songs through given sets of notes on the Piano which leads up to learning 5-finger scales of C and G Major, and A and D Minor. This book is set up for students to write out notes in boxes, which represent beats. Boxes come in sets of 8, 16, and 24 as to give them a good variety of lengths and to prevent overwhelm.

There is also a good mix of titled and untitled songs. Most all songs give students prompts to give them inspiration before writing, and some include a blank title for students to come up with their own. Creativity is the goal here, and students should enjoy the composing process. This book gives students a chance to do so, in small chunks so you can fit them in lessons!

In this part of the book, we will use the C-D-E keys on the piano. Write a song by filling in all the boxes below. Once your boxes are filled, try playing your song to see how it sounds! To finish, title your song!

TITLE: ____

							C

TITLE: <u>A CLEAR DAY</u>

Let's take a walk around the block. What would this sound like in a song? Fill in the boxes below using the C-D-E keys on your piano.

							C

TITLE: <u>THE ROCKING CHAIR</u>

Who wouldn't want to sit back and take a ride in a rocking chair? Come up with a song that sounds like a rocking chair using C-D-E.

							C

TITLE: <u>A WALK IN THE PARK</u>

Still using C-D-E, think of a time when you went to a park or playground. You could spend all day there playing! Put this into a song.

							C

TITLE: ______________________________

							C

TITLE: ______________________________

							C

TITLE: _______________________

The Summertime can be so hot! It makes you want to take a dive into a cool swimming pool. What are the sounds around a pool? Put that into a song with C-D-E keys.

TITLE: <u>FAST CARS</u>

Nothing beats the feeling of taking off on the highway, driving fast, and getting out of town for a little while. What would that feeling be like in a song with C-D-E?

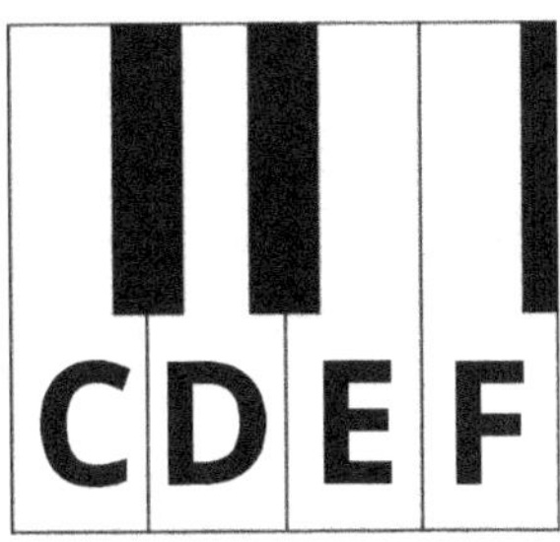

In this part of the book, we will use the C-D-E-F keys on the piano. Write a song by filling in all the boxes below. Once your boxes are filled, try playing your song to see how it sounds! To finish, title your song!

TITLE: ____

<table>
<tr><td></td><td></td><td></td><td></td><td></td><td></td><td></td><td>F</td></tr>
</table>

TITLE: ____

What comes to mind when you hear the word "FAST"? Write a "fast" song using your C-D-E-F keys, then give the song a title!

<table>
<tr><td></td><td></td><td></td><td></td><td></td><td></td><td></td><td>F</td></tr>
</table>

TITLE: <u>STEP RIGHT UP</u>

When the carnival comes to town, how do you feel when you see all the rides, games and food booths set up? Do you step right up?

							C
							F

TITLE: <u>THE TURTLE</u>

Are Turtles fast or slow animals? Have you seen the way they move about? Keep this in mind while you write a song with C-D-E-F.

						F
						F

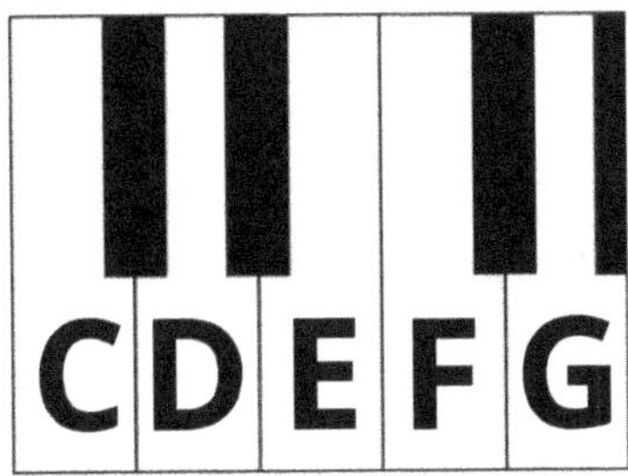

Using the C-D-E-F-G keys, write a song by filling in all the boxes below. Once your boxes are filled, try playing your song to see how it sounds! To finish, give your song a title.

TITLE: ____

							C

TITLE: <u>UP THE HILL</u>

Still using C-D-E-F-G, come up with a song that would make you think of hills, that gently go up and down.

							C

TITLE: <u>HELLO!</u>

You just arrived to your friend or family's home and are happy to see everyone, you shout "HELLO!" at the door. Write this as a song with C-D-E-F-G.

							G
							C

TITLE: _______________________________

When you get inside, you notice that there is a big piece of cake just for you! Write a song that would sound like you enjoying the cake with C-D-E-F-G.

							C
							C

TITLE: <u>YUMMY CAKE</u>

After you've eaten the cake you saw inside your friends house, how did it make you feel? Was it a Yummy Cake?

							G
							C

TITLE: ____

That cake made you very tired. Write a song use C-D-E-F-G that would make you want to take a nap!

							C
							C

TITLE: ________________________________

Now it is time to play a fun game. Are you good with board games? Card Games? Write a fun song with C-D-E-F-G and title it!

							C
							G
							C

TITLE: <u>GOODBYE!</u>

It is now time to say goodbye to your friend or family member, but you know you will see them again. Use C-D-E-F-G to write a song as a "Goodbye!"

							C
							G
							C

In this part of the book, we will use the G-A-B keys on the piano. Write a song by filling in all the boxes below. Once your boxes are filled, try playing your song to see how it sounds! To finish, title your song!

TITLE: ____

							G

TITLE: <u>GREEN GRASS</u>

It's spring time! You open those windows to let some fresh air in and you can smell the green grass growing outside. Put that into a short song with G-A-B!

							G

TITLE: ____

Ever have one of those days when you feel like you're just walking back and forth looking for something? Put that in a song using G-A-B, and give it a title!

<table>
<tr><td></td><td></td><td></td><td></td><td></td><td></td><td></td><td></td></tr>
<tr><td></td><td></td><td></td><td></td><td></td><td></td><td></td><td>G</td></tr>
</table>

TITLE: <u>RELAX</u>

Sometimes, we just need to kick back and relax a little so we can feel ready for anything. What would relaxing be like as a song with G-A-B?

<table>
<tr><td></td><td></td><td></td><td></td><td></td><td></td><td></td><td>G</td></tr>
<tr><td></td><td></td><td></td><td></td><td></td><td></td><td></td><td>G</td></tr>
<tr><td></td><td></td><td></td><td></td><td></td><td></td><td></td><td>G</td></tr>
</table>

In this part of the book, we will use the G-A-B-C-D keys on the piano. Write a song by filling in all the boxes below. Once your boxes are filled, try playing your song to see how it sounds! To finish, title your song!

TITLE: ____

							G

TITLE: <u>DOWN THE HILL</u>

Still using G-A-B-C-D, come up with a song that would make you think of hills, that gently go up and down.

							G

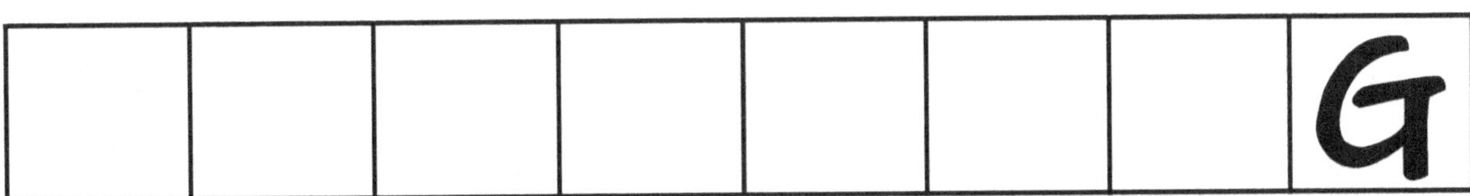

TITLE: <u>A BIG RAINBOW</u>

You look up at the sky and see a really big rainbow after a rainstorm. What do you think a rainbow would sound like?

							D
							G

TITLE: <u>THE BIRTHDAY GIFT</u>

You just got the best gift ever for your birthday and you could not be more excited for it! What would that excitement be like in this song?

							G
							G

On this song, fill in the remaining boxes with any letter and title your song!

TITLE: ____

							G
							G

For this next song, fill in the remaining boxes with any key on the piano and title your song!

TITLE: ____

							G
							G

TITLE: ______________________________

When you're outside, you notice a Dragonfly buzzing past you quickly and caught your attention. Come up with a "Dragonfly Song" with G-A-B-C-D.

							G
							D
							G

TITLE: <u>THE RISING SUN</u>

Before writing this song, take a moment and think of what happens when the sun rises each morning. How does it make you feel?

							G
							D
							G

In this part of the book, we will use the F-G-A-C keys on the piano. Write a song by filling in all the boxes below. Once your boxes are filled, try playing your song to see how it sounds! To finish, title your song!

TITLE: ____

TITLE: <u>CHEESY FRIES</u>

Do you ever feel so hungry, you could eat for days?! Write a song that would make someone think about their favorite food.

In this part of the book, we will use the D-E-F-G-A keys on the piano. Write a song by filling in all the boxes below. Once your boxes are filled, try playing your song to see how it sounds! To finish, title your song!

TITLE: ____

							D

TITLE: ____

Remember a time when a friend said something that made you sad or upset you? Think of that as you write this song using D-E-F-G-A, and give it a title!

							D

							D

On this song, fill in the remaining boxes with any letter and title your song!

TITLE: ____

<table>
<tr><td></td><td></td><td></td><td></td><td></td><td></td><td></td><td>A</td></tr>
<tr><td></td><td></td><td></td><td></td><td></td><td></td><td></td><td>D</td></tr>
</table>

For this next song, fill in the remaining boxes with any key on the piano and title your song!

TITLE: ____

<table>
<tr><td></td><td></td><td></td><td></td><td></td><td></td><td></td><td>D</td></tr>
<tr><td></td><td></td><td></td><td></td><td></td><td></td><td></td><td>D</td></tr>
</table>

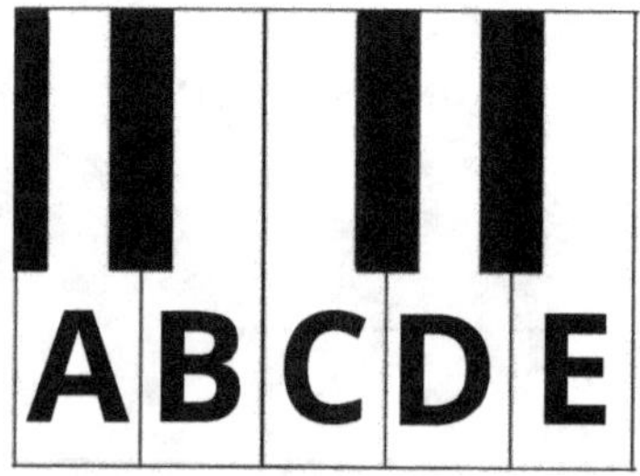

In this part of the book, we will use the A-B-C-D-E keys on the piano. Write a song by filling in all the boxes below. Once your boxes are filled, try playing your song to see how it sounds! To finish, title your song!

TITLE: _______________________________

							A

TITLE: <u>A STORMY SEA</u>

Have you ever seen a river or the sea move when it's windy and storming? It moves quite a bit! How do you think this would sound as a song?

							A

							A

In this part of the book, we will use ALL the piano keys: A-B-C-D-E-F-G.

TITLE: <u>CHEERING UP</u>

Do you remember a time you felt sad, then something happened that made you cheer up and you were happy again? Keep that in mind as you write this song. Between the A's, you can use ABCDE, and between the C's, use CDEFG.

A							A
C							C

TITLE: <u>COMBO NUMBER THREE</u>

On the top row, you can start with: C-D-E-F-G, then use F-G-A-C. On the second row, you can use G-A-B-C-D, or C-D-E-F-G.

C				F		
G						C

On this song, fill in the remaining boxes with any letter and title your song!

TITLE: ____

C							
F				A			
G				C			C

For this next song, fill in the boxes with any key on the piano and title your song!

TITLE: ____

On this song, fill in the remaining boxes with any letter and title your song!

TITLE: ____

<table>
<tr><td></td><td></td><td></td><td></td><td></td><td></td><td></td><td></td></tr>
<tr><td></td><td></td><td></td><td></td><td></td><td></td><td></td><td></td></tr>
<tr><td></td><td></td><td></td><td></td><td></td><td></td><td></td><td></td></tr>
</table>

For this last song, fill in the boxes with any key on the piano and title your song!

TITLE: ____

<table>
<tr><td></td><td></td><td></td><td></td><td></td><td></td><td></td><td></td></tr>
<tr><td></td><td></td><td></td><td></td><td></td><td></td><td></td><td></td></tr>
<tr><td></td><td></td><td></td><td></td><td></td><td></td><td></td><td></td></tr>
</table>

EXTRA PAGES FOR
MORE SONGS!

Hey Composer! The next few pages include boxes that are blank so you can write more songs if you've already filled up this entire book! There are no letters in the boxes so you can write a song using any of the letters of the music alphabet. Happy Composing!

On this song, fill in the boxes with any letter and title your song!

TITLE: ____

On this song, fill in the boxes with any letter and title your song!

TITLE: ____

On this song, fill in the boxes with any letter and title your song!

TITLE: ____

On this song, fill in the boxes with any letter and title your song!

TITLE: ____

On this song, fill in the boxes with any letter and title your song!

TITLE: ____

On this song, fill in the boxes with any letter and title your song!

TITLE: ____

On this song, fill in the boxes with any letter and title your song!

TITLE: ____

<table>
<tr><td></td><td></td><td></td><td></td><td></td><td></td><td></td><td></td></tr>
<tr><td></td><td></td><td></td><td></td><td></td><td></td><td></td><td></td></tr>
</table>

On this song, fill in the boxes with any letter and title your song!

TITLE: ____

<table>
<tr><td></td><td></td><td></td><td></td><td></td><td></td><td></td><td></td></tr>
<tr><td></td><td></td><td></td><td></td><td></td><td></td><td></td><td></td></tr>
</table>

On this song, fill in the boxes with any letter and title your song!

TITLE: ____

On this song, fill in the boxes with any letter and title your song!

TITLE: ____

On this song, fill in the boxes with any letter and title your song!

TITLE: ____

<table>
<tr><td> </td><td> </td><td> </td><td> </td><td> </td><td> </td><td> </td><td> </td></tr>
<tr><td> </td><td> </td><td> </td><td> </td><td> </td><td> </td><td> </td><td> </td></tr>
</table>

On this song, fill in the boxes with any letter and title your song!

TITLE: ____

<table>
<tr><td> </td><td> </td><td> </td><td> </td><td> </td><td> </td><td> </td><td> </td></tr>
<tr><td> </td><td> </td><td> </td><td> </td><td> </td><td> </td><td> </td><td> </td></tr>
</table>

On this song, fill in the boxes with any letter and title your song!

TITLE: ____

<table>
<tr><td> </td><td> </td><td> </td><td> </td><td> </td><td> </td><td> </td><td> </td></tr>
<tr><td> </td><td> </td><td> </td><td> </td><td> </td><td> </td><td> </td><td> </td></tr>
</table>

On this song, fill in the boxes with any letter and title your song!

TITLE: ____

<table>
<tr><td> </td><td> </td><td> </td><td> </td><td> </td><td> </td><td> </td><td> </td></tr>
<tr><td> </td><td> </td><td> </td><td> </td><td> </td><td> </td><td> </td><td> </td></tr>
</table>

On this song, fill in the boxes with any letter and title your song!

TITLE: ____

On this song, fill in the boxes with any letter and title your song!

TITLE: ____

On this song, fill in the boxes with any letter and title your song!

TITLE: ____

On this song, fill in the boxes with any letter and title your song!

TITLE: ____

On this song, fill in the boxes with any letter and title your song!

TITLE: ____

On this song, fill in the boxes with any letter and title your song!

TITLE: ____